WHAT IS MPA? AND

HOW IT ALL

STARTED

BY: MARION GEORGE

THE JOURNEY

THE JOURNEY

A BUSINESS THAT I

STARTED IN THE

FORM OF

ENTREPRENEURSHIP,

, AND BECAME A

LEADER IN THE

COMMUNITY. PLUS, I

BECAME ONE

OUTSTANDING GUY

BY CONTROLLING MY THOUGHTS & GOVERNING MY EGO. IT WASN'T EASY AT ALL, HAVE I BEEN

THIS MINDFUL ALL
MY LIFE, NO! IT'S

BEEN A FUN AND

INTERESTING ONE. A

LOT OF UP, DOWNS

AND BACKFLIPS FOR
17YRS. I AM 32YRS

OF AGE TO THIS

DATE OF
PUBLISHING

THIS BOOK IT'S LATE

IN THE YEAR 2022
AND IT BEEN A

ROCKY BUT

BEAUTIFUL,

WONDERFUL ONE. I

AM FROM NEW

ORLEANS ONE OF

THE MOST

BEAUTIFUL CITIES IN

THE WORLD THAT'S

FULL OF HISTORY,
WHICH DOESN'T GET

MENTION THAT

MUCH. BY GROWING

UP IN DOWNTOWN

NEW ORLEANS I SEEN IT ALL THEY CALL IT

THE GUMBO POTS. IT

HAS BEEN ONE HACK

OF A BLAST. YOU

WANT BELIEVE THE

THINGS I SEEN, AND

EXPERIENCE JUST

BY LIVING DOWN

HERE. OPENED SO

MANY
OPPORTUNITIES AND
DIFFERENT PATHS IN
MY LIFE I COULD'VE
EXPLORED. I

WOULDN'T BE HERE

WRITING OR TYPING

NOTHING IF IT

WASN'T FOR ME

SEEKING THE

AUTHENTIC ME AND THE "INNER ME"

THE SUPREME ME.

I WAS BORN IN 1990

THE SAME YEAR

MARCUS GARVEY

CAME FROM

JAMAICA TO NEW ORLEANS ON A SHIP

THRU THE

MISSISSIPPI RIVER

AND GIVE A

MAGNIFICENT SPEECH. THE PEOPLE

WAS AMAZED TO

SEE HIM AND HEAR

HIM. "MY PARENTS

USE TO ALWAYS
SAY." AND DO YOU

KNOW THEY REFUSE

TO LET HIM OFF THE

SHIP?? HE ONLY

COULD SPEAK FROM

THE DOCK, CRAZY

RIGHT TOUGH TIMES

WHAT HAPPEN TO

JUSTICE AND PEACE.

YOU MUST BE

VERY MINDFUL OF

WHAT YOU SAY THIS

DAYS, CAUSE YOU

MIGHT UPSET THE

WRONG TYPE OF

"POLITICAL PARTY".

"POLITICAL PARTY".

LEFT, RIGHT WHO

CARES THE ELITES

WILL ALWAYS HAVE

THE LAST STEAK
AND WILL ALWAYS

BACK UP THEIR LIES

TO PROTECT THEIR

EXISTENCE. "WHILE

WE ARE THROWING

AWAY THE BONE

FIGHTING

OVER THE GRISTLE

ON THE WAY TO THE

BOTTOM." JUST

SAYING FAMILY! HE

WAS ALSO A BLACK

NATIONALIST THAT

CONTRIBUTE TO

PUSHING THE

MOVEMENT AGAINST

FIGHTING

SEGREGATION ALSO

LIKE MALCOM X AND

MARTIN LUTHER

KING, THEY ALL

WERE VERY GREAT

WERE VERY GREAT

SUPREME NOBLE

MAN. WITH A DESIRE

TO MAKE TO A

CHANGE, TRUE

ARIES BLOOD THE

FIRE WITHIN MAN.

13YRS OLD NOW IN

2002, I GOT THE

URGE FOR MONEY.

SO, MY FRIEND'S AND

I GRABBED AN OLD

BUCKET AND SUM

DASH WASHING

LIQUID, WITH AN OLD

RAG AND STARTED

KNOCKING ON THE
DOORS. OF OUR

NEIGHBORS, DIDN'T

EVEN KNOW WHAT

WE WERE GETTING

INTO OR STARTING

BUT BEFORE YOU

KNOW IT. WE WERE

MAKING A NICE BIT

OF MONEY. IT WAS A

FEW DOORS ON THE
WEEKEND, THEN IT

WAS A FEW

HOUSINGS AND

YARDS. LITTLE

BEFORE WE KNOWN,
OUR URGE FOR

MONEY DID WHAT WE

HAD NO CLUE OF IT

DOING, PLUS WE

WERE JUST
STARTING MIDDLE

SCHOOL. I WAS SO

EXCITED ABOUT US

ACCUMULATING SUM

MONEY. DANG
WHAT'S NEXT? WE

SAID, THEN I TURNED

A SAID "OKAY! ITS

GAME TIME" CUM'ON

I GOT THIS" SO WE

GATHER MORE

GATHER MORE

PRODUCTS FOR

WASHING CARS,

TRUCKS, BUSES &

ETC. I WANTED TO

WASH THE WHOLE

NEIGHBORHOOD IF

YOU LEFT IT UP TO

ME. EVEN THE NEXT

SUBDIVISION. NO

STOPPING NOW, I

WAS EAGER FOR US

TO BE THE BEST. AT

LEAST IN MIND, I

WAS STAVING TO

BECOME DA

GREATEST. JUST

LIKE SNOOP DOGG ON

ON CARWASH THE

MOVIE BUT I TURNED

OUT LIKE EMINEM.

FEW WEEKS PASS BY

BY

AND $200 DOLLARS

A

MONTH WAS NOT

ENOUGH FOR ME, SO

WE JUST HAD TO GET

GET MORE, SO WE

TAKE

A DAY OFF FROM

WORK. I CALLED A

TEAM MEETING, AS

ME AND THE GUYS
WAS TALKING

ABOUT BUSINESS

MOVES AND HOW WE

NEED MORE MONEY.

NOW REMEMBER WE

WERE ONLY AROUND

13 OR 14 YEARS OF

AGE, LITTLE KIDS

BUT I HAD BIG

PLANS, BIG DREAMS,
BIG VISIONS.

BECAUSE FOR SOME

REASON I NEEDED

MORE, WE NEEDED

MORE, IT WAS LIKE

MY NAME WAS

MY NAME WAS

MOORE. "I WAS JUST

EAGER I'M TELLING

YOU." SO AS MY

FRIENDS WERE

DISCUSSING, WHAT

TO DO AFTER THIS

MEETING, SINCE WE

WE'RE TAKING OFF

THAT DAY. "CUM'ON"
I SAID. I WAS

THINKING ABOUT

HOW MUCH DO WE

HAVE TOGETHER

AND NEED TO BUY A
LAWN MOWER SO WE

CAN LEVEL UP BY

THE WEEKEND. WE

STARTED

ANALYZING &
COUNTING OUR

MONEY. BY PUTTING

ALL OUR MONEY

TOGETHER, WE

WERE ABLE TO BUY
A LAWN MOWER AND

AN ELECTRIC WEED

EATER.

NOW IT WAS TIME TO

ACCUMULATE MORE

MONEY. ALL WE

NEEDED TO DO IS

GET FLYERS, MY

FRIENDS' MOM

BOUGHT CARDS AND

FLYERS FOR US. AND

NOW WE WERE IN

BUSINESS, DOING

LAWN CARE AND

CAR WASHES. IT

WAS TIME TO TAKE

OVER THE

NEIGHBORHOOD

"PINKY"!!!

AND WE DID, WEEK

AFTER WEEK,

SUMMER AFTER

SUMMER. WOW!

WE DID IT. THEN LIFE

CHANGE.....

LOST ONE OF MY BIG

BROTHERS

DWIGHT ALLEN

WILLIAMS JR.

MY GUARDIAN

ANGEL NEVER

FORGOTTEN....

love
is the key that opens the heart

hope
is the dream that awakens the soul

peace
is the light that guides the way

faith
is the certainty that sees us through

THREE YEARS

LATER NOW, I'M

REALLY FOCUS ON

SCHOOL. I'M 16

TURNING INTO A MATURED

TEENAGER GOING ON

ON SEVENTEEN.

HURRICANE

KATRINA MOVED US

ALL AROUND. MY

CITY WAS

DESTROYED, OF

COURSE MY

PARENTS HAD TO

RELOCATE TO

ARLINGTON TX. IT

WAS LAME AND

WEIRD TO ME AT

FIRST THEN THINGS

GOT A LITTLE

BETTER. STARTED

TO LIKE THE NEW

LIFE. I THOUGHT IT

WAS THE BORING

LIFE, UPPER CLASS
LIFE SUBURB LIFE

YUCK I WAS A CITY

BOY, PLUS I WAS

STILL UPSET ABOUT

MY FRIENDS AND

BROTHER DEATH SO

IT WAS HARD FOR

ME

TO CONCENTRATE

AND PAY ATTENTION

IN CLASS. MY

TEACHERS DID

THEIR

BEST AND STILL

SHOWED ME HOW TO

BE PATIENT CAUSE I

WAS NOT A NICE

COOKIE, I CAME UP

UNDER A DIFFERENT

DOCTRINE. ALSO

FOLLOWED PEOPLE

WHO HAD PHDS IN

AFRICAN &

AMERICAN STUDIES.

I ALSO STUDY KEMET

KEMET

OR COSMOLOGY SO I

INNER STOOD THE

PHILOSOPHIES OF

WESTERNS VERY

WHILE IN THEM DAYS

& NOW. SO,

TEACHERS AND I DID
NOT AGREE ON

THINGS AT TIMES.

BUT I WAS YOUNG

AND FULL OF

CHASING THE BAG.

NOW UP IN AGE AND

STILL DID NOT LET GO

GO

OF MY PAIN. I USED

SITUATIONS TO LET

MY EGO BUILDS UP
PAIN INSIDE FOR

YEARS, AND IT

DID NOT HELP

NOTHING. I DID NOT

EVEN REALIZE
WHAT WAS GOING

ON, AND WHAT HAVE

TAKING AHOLD OF

ME. I BEEN TO JAIL

FOR PLENTY OF
PETTY CRIMES AND

DRUGS. BUT DO THAT
THAT

MAKE ME A MAN NO.

WE ALL MAKE

MISTAKES OWE UP 2
TWO

THEM NOW AND

MOVE ON TO THE

OTHER DIRECTION. IF
IT IS A POSSIBILITY

OF A NEGATIVE

OUTCOME DON'T DO

IT, I WOULD NOT BE

HERE TODAY LIVING

AN UNREASONABLE

HAPPY LIFE NOW IF I

KEPT UP WITH THE

FOOLISHNESS. AND

DO I STILL CHASE

THE BAG NOPE.

INTUITION IS KEY.

BUT DID I LEARN

THAT OR LISTEN AT

FIRST NOPE. I STILL
DID NOT CARE

BECAUSE I FORGOT

THE YOUNG

BUSINESSPERSON I

WAS

REBELLIOUS, SINCE I

THE FACT THAT I

BUILT ALL THIS PAIN

UP FOR YEARS. MY

EGO WON, YES IT DID.

THEN HERE COME

THE RAIN OR PUT A

"P" ON IT AND YOU

GOT PAIN! I WENT

THROUGH TOUGH

BREAK UPS, BAD

TROUBLED

RELATIONSHIP, LOSS

FAKE FRIENDS

AND FAMILY.

ONCE MY GODCHILD

PASSED AWAY IT
WAS

ENOUGH, PLUS I WAS

DEEP IN THE

STREETS NOW. LIKE

DEEP. WASTE DEEP,

DEEP. MY LIFE WAS

COMPLETELY OFF

TRACK, BUT I WAS

LUCKY ENOUGH TO

FIND SPIRITUALITY.

AND ACCEPT THIS

NEW AWAKEN OF MY

SUPERCONSCIOUS

GOD IN ME. BY

BRINGING BALANCE

AND FORGIVENESS

TO MY LIFE.

IT TURNED MY WAY

OF LIVING

COMPLETELY

AROUND TO BE THE

BUSINESSMAN-

AUTHOR-

ILLUSTRATOR-

ENTREPRENEUR AND

FATHER I AM TODAY.

TODAY. SO, I ENCOURAGE

ENCOURAGE

YOU ALL. ANYBODY

CAN DO IT. I'M

TELLING YOU, "YOU

CAN DO IT" AND THIS

NOT THE MOVIE

WATERBODY HAD TO

DROP A LAUGH. I
LOVE Y'ALL FAMILY

AND WISH Y'ALL

MANY BLESSINGS
AND

ABUNDANCE ON THIS

JOURNEY: NOW I'M
32 WITH 5

BEAUTIFUL KIDS

THAT I CARE ABOUT

WITH EVERY

BREATH

IN MY BODY, AND WE
CAN TALK "ALL

DAY-LONG" BOUT

THAT PART OF MY

LIFE IN THE NEXT

BOOK. BUT I HAD TO

MAKE THIS PART OF

MY JOURNEY CLEAR

FIRST:

I AM FOR THE

PEOPLE, SO I LEAVE

THE EARLY PAST IN

THE PAST CAUSE ITS

EARLY-PAST THAT

KEEP US TRAP WE

STILL OUT HERE

FIGHTING THIS

500YR WAR OF THIS

COLONIALISM. OUR

HISTORY HAS SO

MANY STORIES'

"FACTS" DEPENDS ON

ON

WHERE YOU AT IN

THE WORLD OR WHAT

TIME FRAME YOU ON.

TIME FRAME YOU ON.

ASK ANY HISTORIAN

OR SCHOLAR ITS

ALL-ESOTERIC

KNOWLEDGE. SO,
ANYBODY CAN HAVE

THEIR STORY TOLD.

SO, BY ME SAYING

THAT WE STILL

HAVE WORK TO DO.

WE NEED TO FIX

MANY PROBLEMS,

THAT THE PEOPLE ARE

SUFFERING WITH IN

TODAY'S WORLD.

CAUSE JUSTICE IS

BLIND THE PEOPLE

IS

UNDER THIS MENTAL

SLAVERY AND

DOGMA. BEFORE WE
CAN DO ANYTHING

WE NEED TO FIX

"DAT" THESE NEW

LOST SOULS HAVE NO

NO

CHANCE WE DON'T

STOP THE

COLONIALIZATION

AND THE BIRTH OF

HUMANITY VS
NATURE

AGENDA, THAT'S
KILLING THE PEOPLE

AND NEEDS TO BE

OPPRESSED SO WE

WENT BE

OPPRESSED. NO

MORE AS THE

PEOPLE, SO ALL THE

PEOPLE THAT'S

WILLING TO PROTECT

THYSELF. PLUS

BECOME ONE WITH

GOD. THAT'S ALL

POSITIVE VIBES AND

HIGHLY VIBRATIONS

BEINGS THAT BRING BACK BALANCE TO

THE PLANET. "KAI"

MOTIVATIONAL

SPEECH...   SO

LET NOTHING STOP

YOU. KEEP YOUR

HEAD UP HUSTLE

HARD, WORK SMART

& RIGHTEOUS

BECAUSE YOU HAVE

EYES ALL OVER

WATCHING YOU &
ENERGY VAMPIRES

READY TO KNOCK

YOU OFF YOUR

PEDESTAL. SO, BUILD

BUILD

YOU'RE A FORT

AROUND YOUR

PEDESTAL WITH

GOOD & HONEST

FAMILY MEMBERS

AND LOYAL FRIENDS.

FRIENDS.

NEVER GIVE IN TO

DOUBT, THE

BROTHER OF MISERY.

MISERY. YOU ARE

SMART

ENOUGH TO KNOW &

LEARN. ENOUGH OF

THIS YOU CAN'T,

PROPAGANDA. THE

UNIVERSE IS

MASSIVE AND

ALWAYS ON YOUR

SIDE SO REMEMBERS

TAKE IT ONE DAY AT

AT

A TIME JUST LIKE

MA'AT. BE THE

JUDGE EVERY

SINGLE DAY. SO LIVE

CORRECT NOT

BACKWARDS OR NOT

LIKE SETH. BE YOUR

TRUE AUTHENTIC

TRUE.   AUTHENTIC

CELLS.

THE END! #GENETICS

#CELLFOOD

PEACE LOVE &

BLESSINGS